Little Rama

Rama's Birth And Childhood

DASHARATHA was the king of Koshala kingdom, whose capital was Ayodhya. He had three queens: Kaushalya, Kaikeyi, Sumitra. Due to his long period of childlessness, King Dasharatha performed the Yajna for a son.

Kaushalya gave birth to Rama, Kaikeyi gave birth to Bharata and Sumitra gave birth to twin sons, Lakshmana and Shatrughna.

Among all the four brothers Rama was the

incarnation of Lord Vishnu.

A period of life on earth in
a particular form

Rama plays with Crow

KAKABHUSHUNDI was a great devotee of Shri Rama. He would **loiter** around baby Rama in King Dasharatha's jeweled courtyard.

Stand or wait around without apparent purpose

He felt blessed by glancing at Lord Shri Rama and eating his food. Kakabhushundi kept loitering around Shri Rama's chambers to taste his food crumbs.

Besides, Sri Rama held a malpua sweet in his hand.
Immediately, he expanded his sweetened hand towards Kakabhushundi.
As kakabhushundi moved forward to peck the sweet, shri Rama pulled his hand.

He tried catching the crow with his other hand.

Again, Kakabhushundi pulled back to evade his grasp. This pastime went on for a while.

Kakabhushundi thought, "The lord, whom I worship as the universal master, struggles to catch me."

Immediately, Lord Rama extended his tiny hand toward him. To evade his grasp, Kakabushundi flew with all his might.

However, the lord's hand kept following him.

Finally, Kakaabushundi sat totally exhausted.

Then Shri Rama gulped him.

In his stomach, Kakabhushundi saw the entire cosmic creation. Suns, Moons and countless Stars resided in the lord's stomach.

Eventually, the lord vomited him out of his mouth.

Now, he only saw baby Rama holding a malpua in his hands and smiling sweetly at him.

This is how all of Kakabhushundi's doubts vanished.

Mother Kausalya feeds Rama

KING Dasharata's jeweled courtyard has become the centre of baby Rama's enchanting pastimes.

The laughter of the four princes steal the hearts of all.

Moreover, the Devas reside in Ayodhya to witness Shri Rama's childhood.

Mother Kausalya has already adorned her son. She now wants to call him near for his breakfast.

She holds a small piece of malpua in her hands. Repeatedly, she stretches her hand and requests Shri Rama,

"Son, quickly come here and sit. See, today I have prepared such a delicious breakfast for you.

After breakfast, you
may peacefully go and
play outside with your
brothers and friends."

But now shri Rama wants to trouble his mother with his naughty pranks.

Instead of coming to her, he goes running outside.

Sometimes he also goes running to his mother.

As soon as mother comes to feed him,

he runs away from her and smiles at her.

Mother said, "Son, If you keep troubling like this, then how will I do my other household work? Good children don't act fussy. If you still disobey me, I shall not speak with you."

Now Shri Rama very lovingly sat next to his mother and with his innocent smile mesmerized her.

Shri Rama plays with friends

ONCE Bharata visited mother Kausalya's palace. After venerating mother Kausalya, he touched Shri Rama's feet.

Regard with great respect

Kausalya blessed him.

Thereafter, Shri Rama gave him a warm hug.

Bharat folded his hands and said-

"Oh, blissful one! Now come to play with us. Your dear friends and numerous children are awaiting your presence near the royal gates."

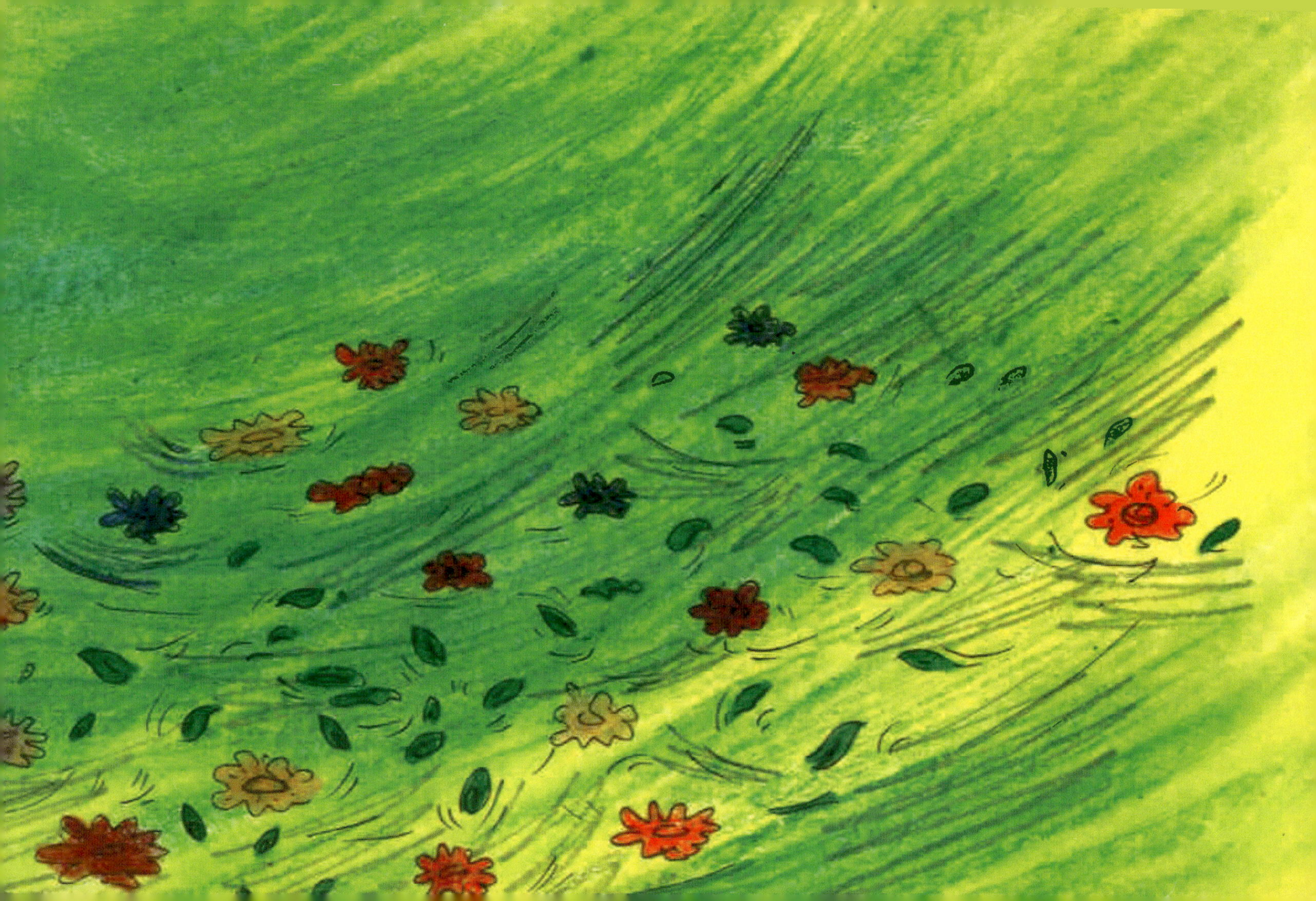

On hearing Bharata's humble appeal,
Sri Rama stood up at once.

Now when shri Rama exits his palace with his friend circle, won't the Ayodhya vasis feast their eyes over his beauteous form.

To hold somebody's attention completely

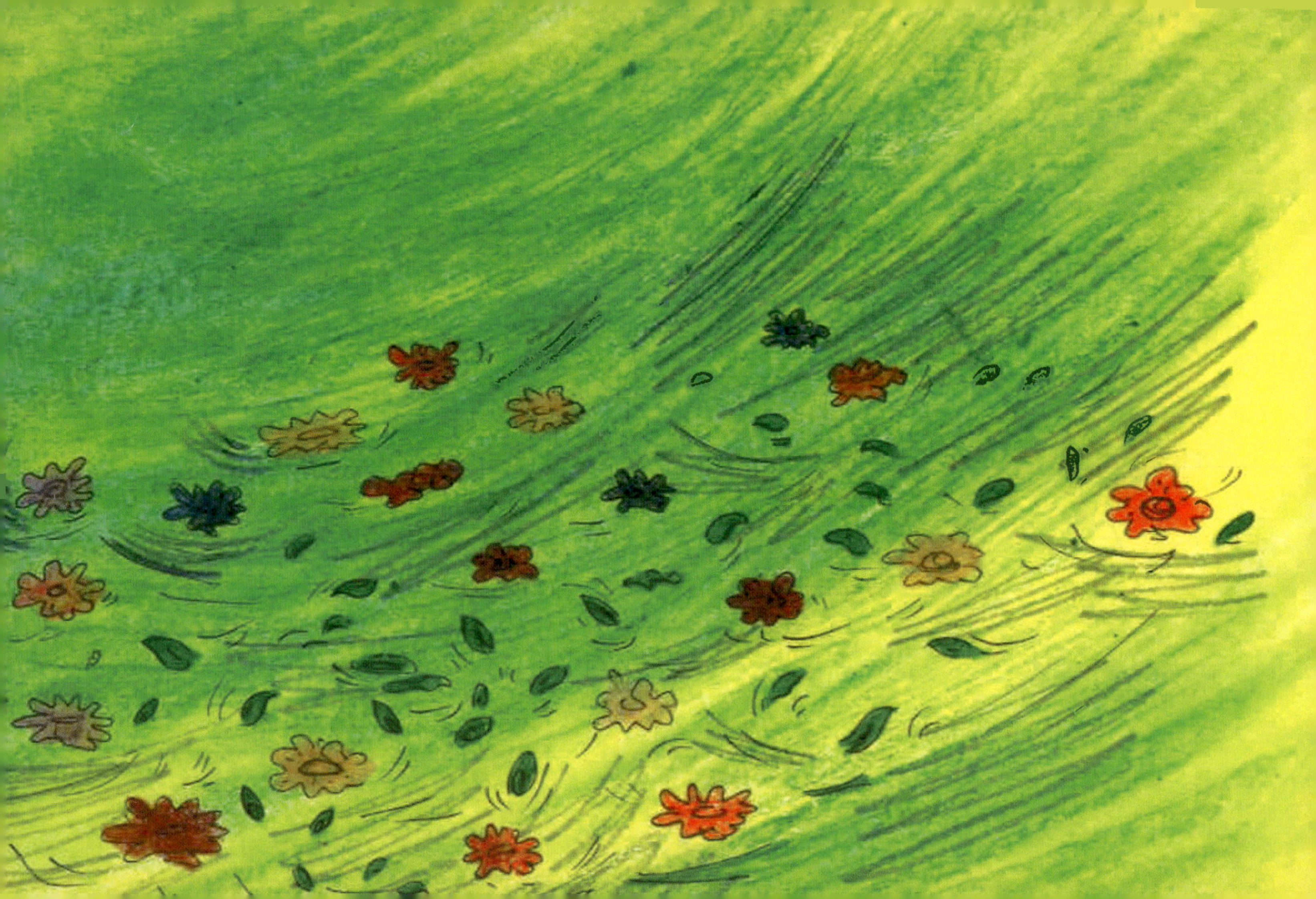

The women of Ayodhya were amazed by his beauty through their windows.

Moreover, they shower flowers on him.

The four brothers, holding a bow in their hands, wearing beautiful cloth, tightening a quicker on their waists. They walk majestically. Studded ornaments dazzle on their bodies.

Lord Rama plays with his friends in the lanes, streets, markets and gardens of Ayodhya.

Kausalya Nandan shri Rama, entertains his friends and audience with his unique playing style.

Shri Rama ventures out on the royal streets, men-women, young-old, all forget their chores and watch him.

An Imprint of Unbound Script

LITTLE RAMA

First Edition - January 2025

ISBN : 978-81-19745-03-6

Publisher : **Unbound Script**
2/41, Ansari Road,
Daryaganj, Delhi - 110002
E-mail : books@unboundscript.com
Website : www.unboundscript.com
Phone No. : 011-35807601

Retold by Kamini Gayakwad
Illustrated by Unbound Script

Printed in India

Price: ₹199/-

Kausalya Nandan shri Rama, entertains his friends and audience with his unique playing style.

Shri Rama ventures out on the royal streets, men-women, young-old, all forget their chores and watch him.

An Imprint of Unbound Script

LITTLE RAMA

First Edition - January 2025

ISBN : 978-81-19745-03-6

Publisher : **Unbound Script**
2/41, Ansari Road,
Daryaganj, Delhi - 110002
E-mail : books@unboundscript.com
Website : www.unboundscript.com
Phone No. : 011-35807601

Retold by Kamini Gayakwad
Illustrated by Unbound Script

Printed in India

Price: ₹199/-